elves, gnomes & other little people

elves, gnomes & other Little people

Coloring Book

John O'Brien

Dover Publications, Inc.
New York

Published in Canada by General Publishing Company, Ltd., 30 Lesmill Road, Don Mills, Toronto, Ontario.
Published in the United Kingdom by Constable and Company, Ltd.

Elves, Gnomes and Other Little People Coloring Book is a new work, first published by Dover Publications, Inc., in 1980.

DOVER *Pictorial Archive* SERIES

International Standard Book Number: 0-486-24049-5

Manufactured in the United States of America
Dover Publications, Inc.
31 East 2nd Street
Mineola, N.Y. 11501

Publisher's Note

For thousands of years people all over the world used to believe that, on land and water, there existed all kinds of small creatures, or "little people," whose activities affected human life in many ways. In part, this was an attempt to explain many mysterious forces of nature which science has now clarified. But even if we no longer believe in these attractive or frightening little beings, we still enjoy the hundreds of stories and poems that have been written about them.

For the present book John O'Brien has given us his new interpretation of a number of well-known "little people." There are traditional "little people" from European folklore: elves, gnomes, goblins, brownies, trolls and leprechauns. There are creatures from modern folklore: the gremlins. There are characters from fairy tales by famous writers: Rumpelstiltskin from the stories of the Grimm Brothers, Thumbelina from the tales of Hans Christian Andersen, and Tom Thumb from narrations by Charles Perrault and others. In addition, there are well-liked characters from such other works of literature as *Gulliver's Travels* by Jonathan Swift, *Rip Van Winkle* by Washington Irving and *A Midsummer Night's Dream* by William Shakespeare.

Four of the pictures have been colored by Mr. O'Brien himself and appear on the covers. But these are just suggestions or samples. In a book as fantastical as this one, why not let your color imagination run away with you?

elves, Gnomes & other little people

Elves used to dance at night in the meadows, where they left bright rings of grass. It was dangerous for a human traveler to be coaxed into joining their dance, for he would most likely pine away and die. Old ballads and folktales contain many different stories about elves.

3

An imp plotting mischief. Imps were young or small devils, or any small super-
natural creatures whose business and pleasure it was to make life difficult for
human beings.

One of the most famous imps was Rumpelstiltskin, who threatened to take away a queen's baby unless she could guess the little man's name. Here he is seen singing and dancing around a fire, sure that he will succeed. But in his song he mentioned his name, someone heard him and told the queen, and she was able to keep her child.

Goblins were playful creatures, but their idea of fun often caused people great trouble. They twisted the hair of sleeping girls, turned themselves into horses and gave people wild and exhausting rides, and performed many other pranks.

Tom Thumb was a little boy, not an elf or gnome, but he was extremely tiny. He had many misadventures with animals because of his size, but he was very smart and got out of every bad situation. Here he is being thrown into the sea, where a greedy fish is waiting to gobble him up.

One of Tom Thumb's most thrilling adventures was in the house of a horrible man-eating ogre. Not only did Tom Thumb escape successfully, but he also managed to run away with the ogre's gold and treasures.

An English ship's doctor, Lemuel Gulliver, was shipwrecked near the islands of Lilliput and Blefuscu, where all the people and their belongings were very small. When he wanted to return home, the people of Blefuscu helped him to repair a broken boat, in which he traveled until he was picked up by a ship.

Pixies liked to guide travelers at night. Here they are helping a man to get safely over a very dangerous bridge. Long ago, when a man got drunk and came home late, and his wife complained, he could say that pixies led him astray and made him get lost.

The Jumblies appear in a poem by the English writer Edward Lear. They lived very far away, they had green heads and blue hands, and they went to sea in a sieve. The people at home thought they would never come back, but they did — after twenty years of exciting travels.

Brownies were good-natured "little people" living in Scotland, where they helped the farmers with many chores. Here they are seen building a stone wall, carrying firewood and water, feeding the chickens, milking the cow, raking, churning butter and thatching the barn roof.

When the Dutch crew of the explorer Henry Hudson played ninepins in the Catskill Mountains of New York State, the sound was heard as thunder in the surrounding hills. Rip Van Winkle found them on his wanderings, and when he drank from their keg of liquor, he fell asleep for twenty years.

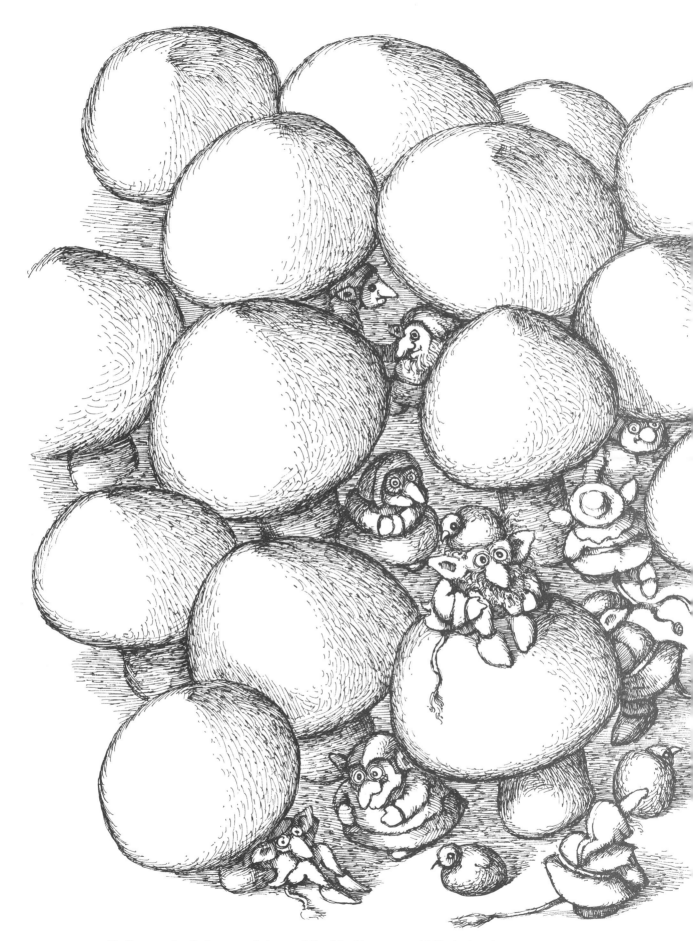

Trolls came in all shapes and sizes and lived inside caves and hills in Sweden, Norway and Denmark. Some of them were monsters, but others were not unfriendly, though it was probably never completely safe to keep them company.

Thumbelina was a tiny girl who was born inside a magic flower. She was kidnapped by toads and beetles, befriended by a field mouse and rescued by a bird that she had saved from freezing. The bird flew with her to a flower garden where she met other flower people like herself and became Queen May Blossom.

Leprechauns led a merry life in Ireland. They looked like little old men and were extremely clever and tricky. If you could manage to catch one, he would hand over his hidden treasure to you.

Here is a leprechaun making shoes for the "little people." Behind him in the hollow
tree is his treasure, in the form of a pot filled with gold.

Gnomes were small creatures who lived inside the earth. When miners dug into hills for metals and coal, the gnomes would frighten them with noise and tricks, and would even cause cave-ins.

Water sprites, also called nixes, were at home wherever there was fresh water, just as the gnomes belonged in the earth. Often nixes would tempt human beings to join them in the river or lake where they lived, and the victims would usually be drowned. The nixes in this picture have the bodies of fishes from the waist down.

29

Gremlins are the most modern of all the "little people" in this book, because their special area of activity is the airplane. Whenever something goes wrong with the motor or other equipment on a plane, a gremlin may be blamed for the trouble.

Some kobolds were house spirits who stayed with one family. Like goblins, these kobolds would play all kinds of tricks on people or else would do them favors, depending on their frame of mind.

Other kobolds lived inside the earth, just like gnomes.

In *The Wonderful Wizard of Oz*, when the cyclone blew Dorothy away from Kansas, she landed in the territory of the Munchkins. These small people, who wore blue clothes and painted their houses blue, were glad to be freed from a wicked witch, who was killed by Dorothy's falling house.

Oberon, a dwarf king, was the leader of the faery people in English folklore. He appears in Shakespeare's famous comedy *A Midsummer Night's Dream*.

Titania, queen of the fairies, is the wife of Oberon in *A Midsummer Night's Dream*.

Puck, or Robin Goodfellow, was a mischievous little goblin or sprite. His greatest pleasure was leading travelers out of their way at night into a ditch or a swamp, although he might also do household chores in return for a dish of cream.

DOVER COLORING BOOKS

FAVORITE ROSES COLORING BOOK, Ilil Arbel. (25845-9) $2.95

FUN WITH SEARCH-A-WORD COLORING BOOK, Nina Barbaresi. (26327-4) $2.50

FUN WITH SPELLING COLORING BOOK, Nina Barbaresi. (25999-4) $2.50

JEWISH HOLIDAYS AND TRADITIONS COLORING BOOK, Chaya Burstein. (26322-3) $2.95

INDIAN TRIBES OF NORTH AMERICA COLORING BOOK, Peter F. Copeland. (26303-7) $2.95

BIRDS OF PREY COLORING BOOK, John Green. (25989-7) $2.95

LIFE IN ANCIENT EGYPT COLORING BOOK, John Green and Stanley Appelbaum. (26130-1) $2.95

WHALES AND DOLPHINS COLORING BOOK, John Green. (26306-1) $2.95

DINOSAUR ABC COLORING BOOK, Llyn Hunter. (25786-X) $2.50

SHARKS OF THE WORLD COLORING BOOK, Llyn Hunter. (26137-9) $2.95

HISTORY OF SPACE EXPLORATION COLORING BOOK, Bruce LaFontaine. (26152-2) $2.95

HOLIDAYS STAINED GLASS COLORING BOOK, Ted Menten. (26062-3) $3.95

FUN WITH OPPOSITES COLORING BOOK, Anna Pomaska and Suzanne Ross. (25983-8) $2.50

DINOSAUR LIFE ACTIVITY BOOK, Donald Silver and Patricia Wynne. (25809-2) $2.50

HISTORY OF THE AMERICAN AUTOMOBILE COLORING BOOK, A. G. Smith and Randy Mason. (26315-0) $2.95

THE VELVETEEN RABBIT COLORING BOOK, Margery Williams and Thea Kliros. (25924-2) $2.95

HEBREW ALPHABET COLORING BOOK, Chaya Burstein. (25089-X) $2.95

COLUMBUS DISCOVERS AMERICA COLORING BOOK, Peter F. Copeland. (25542-5) $2.75

STORY OF THE AMERICAN REVOLUTION COLORING BOOK, Peter Copeland. (25648-0) $2.95

FAVORITE POEMS FOR CHILDREN COLORING BOOK, illustrated by Susan Gaber. (23923-3) $2.95

HORSES OF THE WORLD COLORING BOOK, John Green. (24985-9) $2.95

WILD ANIMALS COLORING BOOK, John Green. (25476-3) $2.95

THE DAYS OF THE DINOSAUR COLORING BOOK, MATTHEW KALMENOFF. (25359-7) $2.95

SMALL ANIMALS OF NORTH AMERICA COLORING BOOK, Elizabeth A. McClelland. (24217-X) $2.95

Paperbound unless otherwise indicated. Prices subject to change without notice. Available at your book dealer or write for free catalogues to Dept. 23, Dover Publications, Inc., 31 East 2nd Street, Mineola, N.Y. 11501. Please indicate field of interest. Each year Dover publishes over 200 books on fine art, music, crafts and needlework, antiques, languages, literature, children's books, chess, cookery, nature, anthropology, science, mathematics, and other areas.

Manufactured in the U.S.A.